Unwritten Pages

Unwritten Pages

Joshua Addison

atmosphere press

© 2025 Joshua Addison

Published by Atmosphere Press

Cover design by Kevin Stone

No part of this book may be reproduced without permission from the author except in brief quotations and in reviews.

Atmospherepress.com

To: Cece

As I reflect on our journey together, I want to take a moment to express my heartfelt apologies for the ways our love and marriage fell short. Though our paths have diverged, please know that the love we shared will always hold a special place in my heart. Thank you for the memories, the laughter, and the lessons learned along the way. I wish you nothing but happiness and fulfillment in your life ahead.

With all my love,
Joshua

Prelude

Unwritten Pages

In the depths of my soul, there are stories untold
Unwritten pages, waiting to unfold
Tears and laughter, joy and despair
A life lived, yet still, so much to share

Ink flows from my heart, as I write through the night
Trying to capture the light, that shines like a beacon bright
The words pour out, like a river's gentle stream
A symphony of emotions, a dream

These unwritten pages, hold secrets and dreams
Fears and hopes, and all that it means
To be human, to love, to live and to grow
A journey of self-discovery, as the pages unfold

May my words find their way, to the hearts that need them most
May they bring solace, and help others find their own voice
For in the unwritten pages, lies a story yet untold
A tale of resilience, of a heart that's made of gold

Chapter One: Childhood Echoes

Eyes

"My dad, a shining star, lost his way
His eyes, once bright, faded into gray
But though his light may have dimmed, his dreams remain
And now, I'll be his eyes, his mind, his guiding flame

I'll hold his vision close, like a precious gem
And make his dreams my own, my heart's greatest theme
With every step, I'll pave the way
For the future he envisioned, the path he'd have me sway

His eyes may be gone, but I'll see for him
And with each glance, I'll honor his whim
His mind, a treasure trove of wisdom and grace
I'll keep it sharp, and hold his place

His dreams, a beacon in the darkest night
I'll make them mine, and shine with all my might
My dad may be gone, but his legacy lives on
In me, his eyes, his mind, his dreams, now forever strong"

My Guiding Light

"Mom, dear mom, my guiding light
I come to you with a heart full of might
I want to say how much I love you so
And apologize for the hard times, I know

I was young and foolish, I couldn't see
The sacrifices you made for me, the love you'd be
I pushed against your guidance, I rebelled and fought
But through it all, you stood strong, never faltering or fraught

You tried your best, even when I thought you were wrong
You showed me love, even when I didn't belong
You held the line, kept me safe, kept me strong
And for that, I thank you, dear mom, all day long

You're a great mom, the best I've ever known
I wouldn't trade you, no matter where I've grown
I love you more than words can say
And I'll be grateful every single day"

Who will cry for the little boy

"Who will cry for the little boy,
Whose innocence was stolen with joy?
Whose cries were drowned out by the sound of pain,
Whose soul was crushed beneath the weight of shame?

Who will mourn the loss of his childhood dreams,
Of safety, love, and gentle streams?
Who will rage against the hands that hurt,
The voices that condemned, the hearts that desert?

Who will heal the scars that mar his soul,
The wounds that, fest'ring, left to unfold?
Who will lift the weight of guilt and shame,
And whisper truth to banish fear's dark flame?

Who will cry for the little boy, now grown,
Still haunted by the ghosts of what was sown?
I will, I will, for he is me, and I am he,
Together we will weep, and let our hearts be free"

Breaking the Chain

"I once was a soul, lost in the dark
Mental health, a battle, a constant spark
But I fought, I rose, I built myself anew
A character, strong, resilient, and true

But now, that strength is tested, worn thin
Tarnished by the weights that I've been forced to pin
The torment, the pain, the constant strife
A never-ending battle, a life without life

I yearn for greatness, for a light to shine
To break free from chains that bind me, to unwind
From negativity's grip, from the darkness that clings
To rise above, to spread my wings

But the weight, the pain, the struggle, it stays
A constant reminder, of the battles I've faced
And though I've built a character, strong and true
I'm still human, still vulnerable, still breaking through"

In Darkness There Is Light

"In darkness, I search for a glimmer of light
A respite from the anguish that pierces through the night
A balm to soothe the wounds that refuse to heal
A gentle touch to calm the turmoil I feel

The weight of sorrow presses me down
A burden too heavy for my soul to bear
I long for a solace that can lift me up
And bring me peace, free from this despair

Perhaps the warmth of love, a tender embrace
A gentle whisper, a comforting grace
The soft caress of hope, a promise to stay
A ray of light to chase the darkness away

Or maybe the gentle lapping of waves on the shore
The soft rustle of leaves, a breeze that soothes once more
The sweet melody of laughter, joy's pure refrain
A world where pain subsides, and my heart can sustain

Whatever it may be, I yearn for the day
When this suffering fades, and I find my way
To a place of serenity, where my soul can rest"

Chapter Two:
Ecstasy of the Heart

Sunset Serenade

"Your smile is like a sunset over the sea
A fiery glow that sets my heart free
Golden rays that dance across your face
A radiant beauty that leaves me in awe and space

Your eyes are like the ocean's waves at dusk
A shimmering blue that beckons me to trust
Your lips, a rosy hue that glows like the sky
A gentle curve that makes my heart want to fly

Your laughter is the sound of seagulls in flight
A joyful melody that fills my life with light
Your presence is the warmth that chases away the night
A sunset lover, shining bright with all your might"

Self-Love

Love, a journey on which we embark, seeking that special heart
But often we forget, the greatest quest is to start
Within ourselves, to grow and to bloom
To become the best version, and let our true selves illume

It's not about finding the right person, but about being the right one
With a heart full of kindness, compassion, and fun
When we focus on our growth, our light shines so bright
And attracts those who resonate, in the most beautiful sight

So let's embrace self-love, and let go of the chase
And recognize that true love starts with our own grace
For when we're whole and content, we'll attract what's divine
And love will find us, in its sweet time

Her Life Is Like a Flame

"Her existence is a radiant blaze, a fierce spark that illuminates her path
A guiding light in the darkest night, leading her through life's turbulent wrath
The weight of her responsibilities is like a raging sea, crashing against her shore
But her unyielding spirit is a sturdy anchor, holding fast and steadfast evermore

Her eyes are like polished gemstones, reflecting the beauty within
A luminous glow that pierces the gloom, revealing a strength that's been forged in the depths of her soul
She aspires to greatness, to leave an indelible mark
But her thoughts can be a tangled web, ensnaring her in a prison of self-doubt and fear

The demands of her profession are like a mighty river, flowing with unrelenting force
But deep within her, a burning ember glows, a fierce determination that refuses to be extinguished or tamed
It's the fire that fuels her resilience, the flame that flickers with every heartbeat
A beacon of hope in the darkness, illuminating the path to her highest aspirations

When the storm has passed, she'll look back and realize
That her inner flame was the beacon that guided her through the turbulent skies

It's the light that illuminated her strength, the fire that forged her unbreakable will
Her life is a radiant blaze, a shining testament to the power that lies within"

Lipstick

"Forgive me if I trip and stumble,
for I know not how to truly speak to you as well.
My words are awkward, unrefined,
like untended gardens, overgrown and left to dwell.

I am clumsy, and my phrases falter,
like a painter's brushstrokes, uncertain and altered.
But let me take you by the hand,
and guide you through the uncharted terrain of my heart.

And kiss you instead,
let the soft touch of our lips paint for you a visual,
a masterpiece of emotions, vibrant and true,
that my shy and clumsy heart cannot.

Your lipstick lingers, passion's hue,
on my skin, a memory that lasts awhile.
In that gentle kiss, I'll convey,
the depths of my soul, the dreams I've made.

Our lips, a canvas, tender and warm,
a love letter written, without a single word to form.
And remember that forgiveness is warm,
like the tears running down your beautiful cheeks,

washing away the doubts, the fears, the pain,
leaving only love's pure, unblemished stain.
As you're standing in the rain,
think of me, and the love we've made.

The droplets on your skin, like diamonds shine,
reflecting our love, in all its beauty, divine.
Let the rain's melody serenade,
our hearts, beating as one, in perfect harmony.

In every raindrop, hear my whisper,
'I love you,' echoing, forever and always."

Close Enough to Hurt

"Two bodies, side by side, yet worlds apart
Anger ignites, voices raise, a stormy heart
But why the shouting, the raised tone, the fight?
Is it not because our hearts, are lost in flight?

We stand so close, yet miles away
Emotions locked, words unspoken, all day
The chasm grows, the void expands
Until our words become weapons, in demand

We shout to bridge the gap, to reach the shore
To make our voices heard, as love seems poor
But in the noise, we drown the truth
And in the chaos, our hearts lose their youth

So let us step closer, hand in hand
And listen to the whispers, of a tender land
For when our hearts align, our voices soft and low
We'll find the love we seek, in each other's glow."

Chapter Three: When Love Fails

Rivers Lament

"A calm, cool face of a river, asks me for a kiss.

But I can't bear to give it, my heart is in shambles.

The water's edge, a cruel reminder, a haunting echo

Of the love that once was, of the heart that's now broken.

I turn away, my eyes brimming with tears.

The river's lips, a mocking smile, a hollow comfort

In this moment, all is lost, all is in shards.

The world crashes down, and it's just me, alone and scarred.

The river's kiss, a bitter taste, a heartbreak's sting

A calm, cool face of a river, a cold, unfeeling thing."

Remember Still

"I still remember the way my body would react when thoughts of you crossed my mind. It was as if my brain had memorized the sensations, the feelings, the emotions that came with being intimate with you. Like an open door that I forgot to lock, you would slip into my thoughts, and I'd be transported back to our moments together.

Even now, I still hold the keys to your heart, and mine. I don't mean to intrude, but my thoughts take me back to our time together, and before I know it, I'm driving down your street, reliving memories we shared. The visits may be fewer, but the memories remain, a bittersweet reminder of our love.

I'm learning to cherish those moments, even as I move forward. You may not be a part of my present, but you'll always be a part of my past, and my heart."

Fri(ENDS)

"Friendship, a bond so fragile, yet so strong
A thread that weaves our hearts together, all day long
But like a delicate vase, it can shatter and fall
Leaving us with shards of memories, and a heart that's lost its call

We once laughed and dreamed, in each other's embrace
But now, the silence is deafening, a hollow space
Where did we go wrong? Was it fate, or just a mistake?
Did we grow apart, or did our love just fade?

I miss the you, who once knew me so well
The one who saw my soul, and made my heart swell
But now, you're just a memory, a ghost in my mind
A reminder of what we had, and what we left behind

But even in loss, I'll hold on to the love we shared
The moments we cherished, the laughter we dared
For though our friendship ended, in tears and in pain
It once was a gift, a treasure, a bond that will remain"

To the Ends of Earth

"Oh, the distance I would travel
To retrace the steps of our past
To relive the moments we shared
And make them last

I would walk to the ends of the earth
Through deserts hot and oceans wide
Through mountains steep and valleys deep
To find my way back to your side

For the chance to love you once more
To hold you close and adore
To make up for the mistakes I made
And show you the love I've never faded

I would traverse the world's vast space
To earn a second chance at our embrace
To prove that my heart beats for you alone
And that my love will forever be your home

So if the path ahead is long and dark
Know that my footsteps will never falter or shirk
For I would walk to the end of the earth
To love you again, and give you new birth"

Tears

"Tears fall like rain, a never-ending stream
A daily ritual, a heart that screams
For change, for growth, for a life anew
A marriage transformed, a love renewed

I weep for the me I once knew
A shadow of a soul, a heart so few
Longing to break free, to shed the skin
Of insecurities, of fears within

But the days blend, the pain remains
The ache of stagnation, the weight of chains
And still I cry, a river wide and deep
A plea for transformation, a soul to keep

But in the tears, a glimmer shines
A glimpse of hope, a heart that aligns
With strength and grace, a will to rise
To face the fears, to shape the skies

And though the tears may fall again tomorrow
I'll hold on tight to the hope I borrow
For change is coming, it's on the horizon
A new dawn breaks, a new me emerges"

The Writing Is on the Wall

"How do I live, how do I breathe
When you're not here, I'm suffocating
My heart beats slow, my soul can't flee
Without you, my love, I'm perpetually weighted

I long to feel love course through my veins
To be alive, to be whole again
But without you, all I feel is pain
A hollowness that gnaws, a grief that remains

Is this where I give it all up?
Surrender to the emptiness, the hurt?
Or do I hold on, and keep on loving?
Even when it feels like my heart is rusting

The writing is on the wall, it's clear to see
My love for you, it's all that's left of me
Without you, I'm just a shadow of myself
A faint outline, a mere ghostly wealth"

Chapter Four: Beyond Vows, Beneath Skins

Click Click Boom

"My heart beats like a drum, a rhythm of pain
A memory triggers, and I'm back in the game
Nostalgia creeps in, like a thief in the night
Stealing my peace, and igniting the fight

The love we had, a fire that once burned bright
Now reduced to embers, a lingering light
But I can't help myself, I'm drawn to the flame
Risking heartbreak, playing a dangerous game

Click click boom, the sound of my heart exploding
Click click boom, the pain I can't seem to outgrow
I thought I was healing, but the wound is still raw
The ghost of our love, a weight I can't withdraw

I'm stuck in the past, reliving what we had
A bittersweet nostalgia, driving me mad
I know I should move on, but I can't let go
The memories haunt me, a ghostly echo

Click click boom, the sound of my heart breaking
Click click boom, the pain I can't stop making
I'm trapped in this cycle, a vicious routine
Trying to fill the void, but the pain remains supreme"

Reflections of a Lost Bloom

"I wish I had told her how much she meant to me when we were still together, and how much I appreciated the water she poured into me, nurturing me through all the moments we shared.

She had planted herself within me, and together we were meant to bloom. But I broke free, leaving her behind. I watched as she poured more water into me than she did herself, until she was drained and lost herself in the process.

If only I had kept God in our garden, maybe our bond would have grown strong like an oak tree _ roots deep, foundation unshakeable. Our connection would have flourished from seed to maturity.

Instead, I became the rot that caused our garden to wither, leaving it dry and barren.

If only I would have poured water into her, as she did for me, our roots might still be entwined. But sadly, I must accept that she's found new soil to bloom in, and I must learn to rejoice in her re-growth, even without our shared roots."

Tabby Cat

"Starting out soft and gentle, but with claws that scratch
It begins with a whisper, a tender touch, a warm caress
But can turn into a hiss, a growl, a dangerous game of cat and mouse

I saw him today, a young man entranced
By a woman with a captivating presence
Her hair was a wild tangle of pink
Her ass curved in ways that seemed almost impossible

He was blinded by his desire for her
Couldn't see the danger signs, the warning bells
She was a master of manipulation
Playing games with his heart, with his emotions

Her eyes gleamed with a feline intensity
Her smile was a weapon, a tool to disarm
She was a predator, and he was her prey
Unaware of the danger that lurked beneath her charm

She wasn't honest about her intentions
But he was too caught up in the thrill to listen
She was already planning her next move
Leaving him broken and shattered, like a toy she'd discarded

She was unpredictable, but charismatic
One moment sweet, the next moment deadly
He was caught in her claws, unable to escape
A pawn in her game, a plaything for her to bat around

I wanted to warn him, to tell him to beware
But he was too far gone, too caught up in her snare
So I just watched, as they walked by
A tabby cat and her prey, a dangerous game that would end in heartbreak"

Lust

"As the day bleeds into night, my defenses crumble, and you pulled the rug from beneath me. I don't know; I guess I kind of liked how you numbed the pain. I was getting used to someone like you.

Stepping into the hush of the evening, I found solace in your presence, a refuge from the depths that haunt me. Your touch ignited a faint glow, illuminating the contours of my soul.

In the silence, I discovered comfort in your embrace, a sanctuary from the weight that bears down on me. Your voice was a gentle whisper, easing the ache within.

But with every passing night, the pain seeps back in, like a tide reclaiming the shore. I'm left to confront the hurt, the vulnerability, and the ache.

Yet, I'm drawn to the familiar comfort of your presence, even as it undermines my resolve. I'm torn between the need to heal and the temptation to escape the pain.

I'm hurting, but I'm accepting it. The ache has become a constant companion, a reminder of the fragility of lust and the resilience of my heart.

In this fragile dance, I'll remember the moments we shared, even as I acknowledge the impermanence of our connection."

Chapter Five:
Social Barriers

Good vs. Nice

We often conflate being nice with being good
But the truth is, they're not quite the same mood
Being nice is about pleasing others, avoiding conflict
But being good is about standing up for what's correct

Nice people might smile and nod, avoiding strife
But good people will speak out against injustice in life
Nice people might turn a blind eye to wrongdoing
But good people will take a stand, even if it's not convenient

Don't get me wrong, niceness has its place
But it's shallow and hollow, a superficial grace
Goodness runs deeper, it's a character trait
A commitment to kindness, empathy, and fair play

Let's strive to be good, not just nice
Let's stand up for what's right, even if it's not nice
Let's be the change we want to see
And embody the goodness that the world needs

Growing as a Man

"Yo, listen up, let me tell you something real
Growing as a man, it's a journey I must feel
Can't stay stagnant, gotta push forward, no doubt
Despite the challenges, gotta keep moving, no rout

Cause life's too short, and time's too precious
To be held back by fear, or comfort, or nervous
Gotta face my demons, and overcome the stress
Gotta be the man I know I'm meant to be, no less

Growing as a man, it's not just about me
It's about the people who look up to me, see
My family, my friends, my community, they need
A man who's strong, who leads, who takes the lead

So I gotta rise above, gotta be the best
Gotta push through struggles, and put my fears to rest
Gotta grow, gotta learn, gotta adapt and evolve
Gotta be the man I know I'm meant to be, no need to prove

So I'll keep pushing forward, no matter the test
Cause growing as a man is the best way to be blessed"

Toxicity Within the Male

"Brotherhood, a bond that's meant to be strong
But too often, it's a poison that lingers all day long
We tear each other down, with words that cut deep
A constant competition, where egos never sleep

We mock each other's vulnerability, with sneers and with scorn
Afraid to show weakness, lest we be torn
From the tribe, from the pack, from the brotherhood's grasp
So we hide behind masks, and pretend to be tough, at last

But the toxicity festers, like a wound that won't heal
It spreads to our relationships, our families, our streets
We perpetuate cycles of pain, of aggression and shame
And wonder why our friendships rarely bear the same name

Enough! Let's break this curse, this vicious cycle of hate
Let's learn to lift each other up, before it's too late
Embrace our vulnerability, our emotions, our hearts
For true strength lies in love, not in tearing each other apart"

Undefined

"Be wary of those who try to define
Your identity, with a glance or a line
They see only surfaces, not the depths within
And yet, they dare to tell you who you've been

They don't know your story, your struggles, your dreams
They haven't walked your path, or felt your extremes
But still, they claim to know just what you need
And try to box you in, with their limited creed

Don't let them label you, don't let them confine
Your beauty, your complexity, your shining design
You are more than what they see, more than what they say
You are a universe, vast and uncharted way

So stand tall, and claim your own identity
Don't let others tell you who you're meant to be
You are the author of your own life's tale
Write your own story, and never let it fail"

Final Chapter: Beneath the Surface

Goldfish

"We were like goldfish swimming in a bowl, our lives seemingly carefree as we circled around each other. Tony was the brightest fish among us, always smiling and lighting up the room with his infectious energy. He'd urge us to 'have fun and smile,' and we'd follow his lead, mesmerized by his goofy charm. But behind his contagious smile, Tony was secretly battling monstrous inner demons, his thoughts raging like a raging sea.

As we swam alongside him, we had no idea he was struggling to stay afloat. His smile, though radiant, was also a mask that hid his pain. And then, one day, Tony's light flickered out. He was gone, leaving us stunned and grief stricken. The remaining four of us continued to swim, trying to find our way without our bright friend. But even as we smiled and lived our lives, we knew that our bowl would never be the same without Tony's sparkle."

About Atmosphere Press

Founded in 2015, Atmosphere Press was built on the principles of Honesty, Transparency, Professionalism, Kindness, and Making Your Book Awesome. As an ethical and author-friendly hybrid press, we stay true to that founding mission today.

If you're a reader, enter our giveaway for a free book here:

SCAN TO ENTER
BOOK GIVEAWAY

If you're a writer, submit your manuscript for consideration here:

SCAN TO SUBMIT
MANUSCRIPT

And always feel free to visit Atmosphere Press and our authors online at atmospherepress.com. See you there soon!

About the Author

JOSHUA ADDISON is an Army veteran residing in Washington State. Currently pursuing graphic design courses, he channels his creativity and experiences into his studies. Joshua discovered poetry writing as a powerful outlet for self-expression, allowing him to articulate his thoughts and emotions in a unique way. His military background has instilled in him a strong sense of discipline and dedication, which he applies to both his academic pursuits and his writing. With a passion for visual arts and literature, Joshua strives to create meaningful connections through his work, blending his life experiences with his artistic endeavors.

www.ingramcontent.com/pod-product-compliance
Lightning Source LLC
LaVergne TN
LVHW041637070526
838199LV00052B/3410